Alan and the
ALIEN

Peter Leigh

Published in association with
The Basic Skills Agency

Hodder & Stoughton

A MEMBER OF THE HODDER HEADLINE GROUP

Acknowledgements
Cover: Oisin McGann
Illustrations: Oisin McGann

Orders: please contact Bookpoint Ltd, 130 Milton Park, Abingdon, Oxon OX14 4SB. Telephone: (44) 01235 827720, Fax: (44) 01235 400454. Lines are open from 9.00 - 6.00, Monday to Saturday, with a 24 hour message answering service. Email address: orders@bookpoint.co.uk

British Library Cataloguing in Publication Data
A catalogue record for this book is available from The British Library

ISBN 0 340 84898 7

First published 2002
Impression number   10 9 8 7 6 5 4 3 2 1
Year   2007 2006 2005 2004 2003 2002

Copyright © 2002 Peter Leigh

All rights reserved. No part of this publication may be reproduced or transmitted in any form or by any means, electronic or mechanical, including photocopying, recording, or any information storage and retrieval system, without permission in writing from the publisher or under licence from the Copyright Licensing Agency Limited. Further details of such licences (for reprographic reproduction) may be obtained from the Copyright Licensing Agency Limited, of 90 Tottenham Court Road, London W1P 9HE.

Typeset by SX Composing DTP, Rayleigh, Essex.
Printed in Great Britain for Hodder & Stoughton Educational, a division of Hodder Headline Plc, 338 Euston Road, London NW1 3BH by Athenaeum Press, Gateshead, Tyne & Wear.

About the Play

The People
- **Alan**
- **Kolpan**, the alien

The Place
By a small lake. There is a wood by the lake.

What's happening
Everything is quiet. **Alan** *is fishing.*

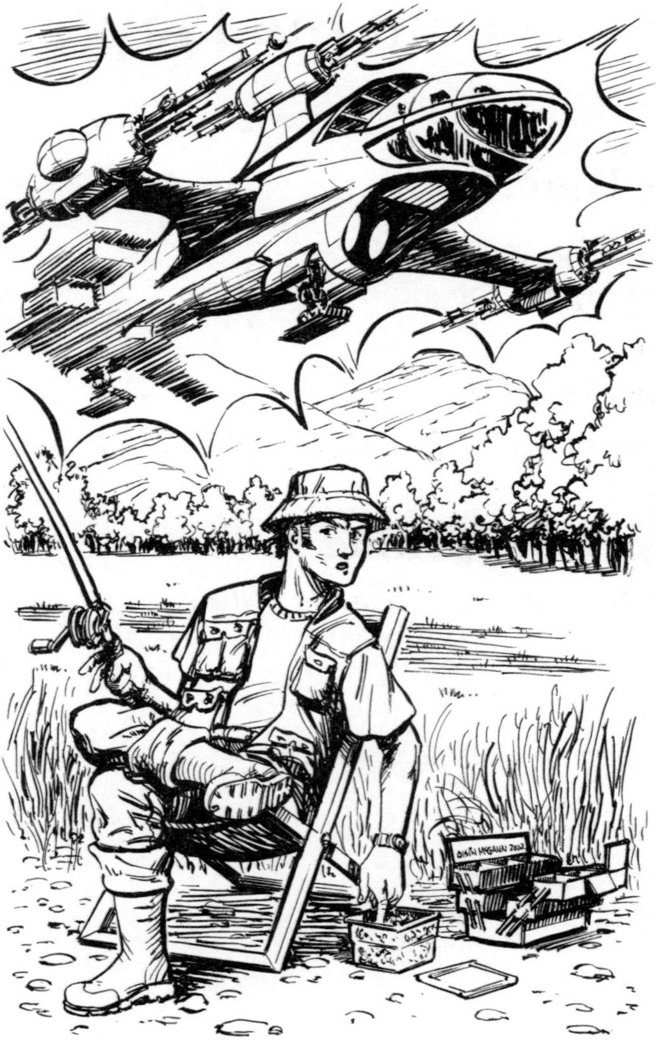
OISÍN MCGANN 2002

Alan This is great. This is so good.

An hour passes.

This is so exciting.

Another hour.

Never a dull moment
when you're fishing.
I need some more maggots.

He reaches down to a box beside him.
Suddenly there is a bright flash.
A spaceship lands just behind him.

Good heavens!

The spaceship shuts off its engine.
Alan stares at it. A hatch opens in
the spaceship. **Kolpan** *gets out.*

Kolpan Godden splatter!
Zeeteedrew petifab
di splotzer, pitihoo!

Alan What?

Kolpan fiddles with some knobs on his belt.

Kolpan Grod mogging!
Fuve mimmion looters of witter, plose!

Alan What? What are you saying?

Kolpan fiddles a little more.

Kolpan Good morning!
Five million litres of water, please!
Sorry about that!
It's these new translators – they take a little tuning in.

Alan still stares at him.

Five million litres of water, please.
What's the matter?
Can't you — ?

He suddenly breaks off.

Oh I'm sorry,
this is self-service, isn't it?
Tell me where the pumps are,
and I'll fill her up myself.

He points to a nearby wood.

Is that a cafe?
Is there a toilet there? I'm busting.

Alan still just stares.

	Hello? Anyone at home?
	I said, is this self-service?
Alan	No-o . . . it's not . . . self-service.
Kolpan	Oh well. Will you fill her
	up for me, then?
Alan	Are . . . are you from space?
Kolpan	What? Oh yes, from Zirgon.
	Just round the corner from here.
	Well come on, then. Chop, chop!
	I haven't got all day, you know.

Alan	Are you really from space?
Kolpan	Yes! Of course I am. From Zirgon, like I told you. Now, can I have five million litres of water, *please*?
Alan	This . . . this isn't a service station.
Kolpan	Isn't it? It looks like one.

He points to the lake . . .

There are the tanks,

. . . and to the wood

and there's the cafe.
Mmm, I'm starving.
Those trees look really good.
I'd love a fried tree now,
with sawdust ketchup.

Alan It's . . . it's not a cafe,
and this isn't a service station.
There are no service stations here.

Kolpan What, none at all? There must be! Look at the map here.

He pulls something out.
It looks like a long piece of string.

See, I came down
past the Milky Way.
You should have seen
the traffic there –
there were mega hold-ups,
at least three light years long.

	The starway was being repaired – all the planets were coned off. Oh look, I can see what I've done. I turned left after Ursa Major instead of right. So instead of going on to the S25 I've come down this dead-end. Can you help me get back on to the starway? Look, if I take the next right, round this black hole here, and left at that solar system, can I get back just here . . . ?
Alan	I don't know.
Kolpan	Well, if you look at the map . . .
Alan	No, I don't know anything about space. You see, this is just too much. I'm a bit shocked. I've never met one before.
Kolpan	One what?

Alan	An alien.
Kolpan	I'm not an alien.
	I'm a Zirg from Zirgon.
Alan	No, I mean not *anyone*.
Kolpan	What, not even the Zogs
	from Zogon?
Alan	No.
Kolpan	Or the Kads?
	You must have met
	the Kads from Kadron.
	There are millions of them.
Alan	No, not any of them.
Kolpan	What kind of a place is this, then?
Alan	That's the point.
	We haven't seen anyone from space.
	We don't believe in spacemen.
	Well, some people have said
	they've seen UFOs,
	and little green men,
	but no one believes them.
	That's why this is so amazing.

He is starting to get excited.

	This is the most important thing that's ever happened, and I'm right in the middle of it.
Kolpan	What? You're kidding! I mean – what's your name, by the way?
Alan	Alan.
Kolpan	Well Al, I mean you don't have to go very far, just over to the next galaxy, and you'll see a thousand different people.
Alan	But I've never been in space. I've never been off the ground – well, except for a fortnight in Ibiza.
Kolpan	What? Never been off the planet?
Alan	No, none of us have.

	Except for one or two astronauts. They've been to the moon and back.
Kolpan	The moon? That bit of rock up there?
Alan	Yes.
Kolpan	There and back? And that's all? My back garden's longer than that. Oh, I just can't believe this. You've never been in space, you've never met anyone from space, and no one from space has ever been here! This is amazing! I've discovered an undiscovered planet.
Alan	Well, it's not undiscovered. We've discovered it.
Kolpan	This is fantastic. I'll be famous all over the universe.

	They'll call me Kolpan the Great – that's my name, by the way. Kolpan the Great Explorer.
Alan	There's nothing left to explore – we've explored it all.
Kolpan	Perhaps they'll name it after me. 'Kolpanland' – what do you think? Or maybe just 'Kolpo'?
Alan	It doesn't need a name —
Kolpan	Too stuffy, maybe. I know – 'Planet Paradiso'. How about that? Yes, I like that.
Alan	Look, it's called Earth, all right? It's not Kolpo or Paradiso or anything like that. It's called Earth. It's ours. We called it that. It's our home.
Kolpan	All right, all right! Don't get upset. Hey Al, listen to this – *(putting on a funny voice)*

	'Greetings – Earthling!
	We – come – in – peace –
	and – friendship!
	Take – me – to –your – leader!'
	(laughing to himself)
	Or this –
	'May – the – force – be – with – you!'
Alan	Oh, very funny!
Kolpan	I'm sorry, but I just can't
	get over it.
	I've discovered an
	unknown world.
	Me! Kolpan the Zirg!
	I've found a backward people,
	living like savages —
Alan	Wait a minute, wait a minute!
	Who are you calling backward
	and savages?
Kolpan	Listen, Al!
	I've just had a great idea.
	An undiscovered planet like this
	could make big money.

Al, these days the universe
is a small place,
and it's getting smaller
by the minute.
People will pay a fortune
to get away from it all.
I mean, take the Kads for example.
They're living two million
to the square metre at the moment.
They'd give an arm and a leg
for somewhere like this.
Well, in the Kads' case,
six or seven arms and legs.

Alan But I don't want them here,
with or without arms and legs.

Kolpan Al, it's progress,
and you can't stop progress.
Between you and me, Al,
this whole area is ripe
for development.
And we can be in on
the ground floor.

	You and me, Al. Together.
We can make a fortune.
I mean, a few hotels right here,
and a Kad would pay . . .
I don't know . . .
a half a bucket of sand a week.
Alan	What?
Kolpan	Think of that, Al.
That's a whole bucket in a fortnight.
And that's just one Kad.
Think what you can get for that.
Alan	Half a bucket of sand?
Kolpan	What?
You mean it should be
a whole bucket?
Wow, you're thinking big.
Perhaps you're right.
We shouldn't be too cheap.
Alan	I don't want a bucket of sand.
Kolpan	What? A bright young man
like you could go a long way
on a bucket of sand.

Alan	No, a bucket of sand doesn't mean anything to me.
Kolpan	Al, Al, I hear what you're saying. I know where you're coming from. But I live in the real universe, Al, and . . .
Alan	But sand isn't worth anything.
Kolpan	Well, yes, I know. Not compared to the important things in life like family and friends, the sky at night, a beautiful sunset, but even so . . .
Alan	No, a bucket of sand really isn't worth anything. There's lots of sand around. There's a building site over that hill where you could get a ton of it.

Kolpan	WHAT? Do . . . do you mean . . . you have a lot of sand here?
Alan	Of course we do. We've beaches full of sand, deserts of it.
Kolpan	So . . . so . . . wait a minute, let me get this right. Do you mean that sand is as common here as, say, diamonds are on Zirgon?
Alan	DIAMONDS?
Kolpan	Yes, you know the stuff. You can't get rid of it. I must have some around somewhere. *(reaching into his spacesuit)* It gets into all your pockets. Ah, here we are.

He pulls out a small handful of diamonds.

Alan gulps.

Alan These diamonds . . .
They're common on Zirgon?
Kolpan Common?
They're all over the place.
They get in your hair,
stuck in your shoe.
You can't get rid of them.
Alan Well then . . .
(smiling brightly)
. . . what did you say your name
was? Kolpan, was it?

Alan	Well, Kolp – I think we can come to some agreement.
Kolpan	Al, I knew you'd see sense. You won't regret this, I promise you. We can set up a tourist business right here. We just need to check the future to make sure everything's ok.
Alan	What?
Kolpan	Check the future.
Alan	How do we do that?
Kolpan	Time travel, of course.
Alan	Time travel?
Kolpan	Yes.
Alan	Can you do time travel?
Kolpan	Of course I can – everyone can.

He looks at Alan closely.

	Do you mean *you* can't?
Alan	No.
Kolpan	Really?

Alan	Yes.
Kolpan	What – not just pop into the future or the past for a bit of a break?
Alan	No.
Kolpan	But if you can't go into the future, how do you know if you're doing the right thing now?
Alan	*(confused)* I'm sorry?
Kolpan	Look, if you want to go somewhere you don't start out without knowing how to get there, not even on a tiny place like Earth. It's the same with time – if you're doing something now, and you don't know how it's going to turn out, how do you know if it's the right thing to do? It's like walking down a street not knowing where it goes to.
Alan	Well, you just do it even if you don't know.

Kolpan	And how do you change things in the past so that they're all right in the present?
Alan	Well, you can't.
Kolpan	That's terrible! Not knowing the past or the future! I couldn't live like that. I'm glad I'm not you.
Alan	It's not that bad. In fact, it's pretty good. I'm glad I don't know everything that's going to happen in the future.
Kolpan	Look, I must have a closer look. I'm just going to go backwards and forwards a bit. I'll be back in a minute.

Kolpan suddenly disappears.

Alan	What . . . ? What do you mean . . . ?

Kolpan suddenly reappears.

Kolpan Sorry about that.
Well that was very interesting,
I must say.
Those dinosaurs, they
were something.
I wouldn't like to meet one of them
on a dark night.
And then the Egyptians –
I spent ages with them.
They made me their sun-god.
They were trying to build
these circles.
'Ra,' I said – that's their king
by the way –
'Ra – circles are no good.
It's got to be pyramids.'
I think he took the hint.

| | Which is more than
that Harold did.
'Get some shades fitted
to your helmet,' I told him.
'You need the protection.'
But did he listen? No!
And then . . . |
| --- | --- |
| **Alan** | Wait a minute, wait a minute.
You were only gone for
a second or so.
How come you did
all these things –
met the Egyptians, saw the
dinosaurs, and so on. |
| **Kolpan** | Al – it's time travel. |
| **Alan** | So? |
| **Kolpan** | Well, seconds here can be years
in time travel. |

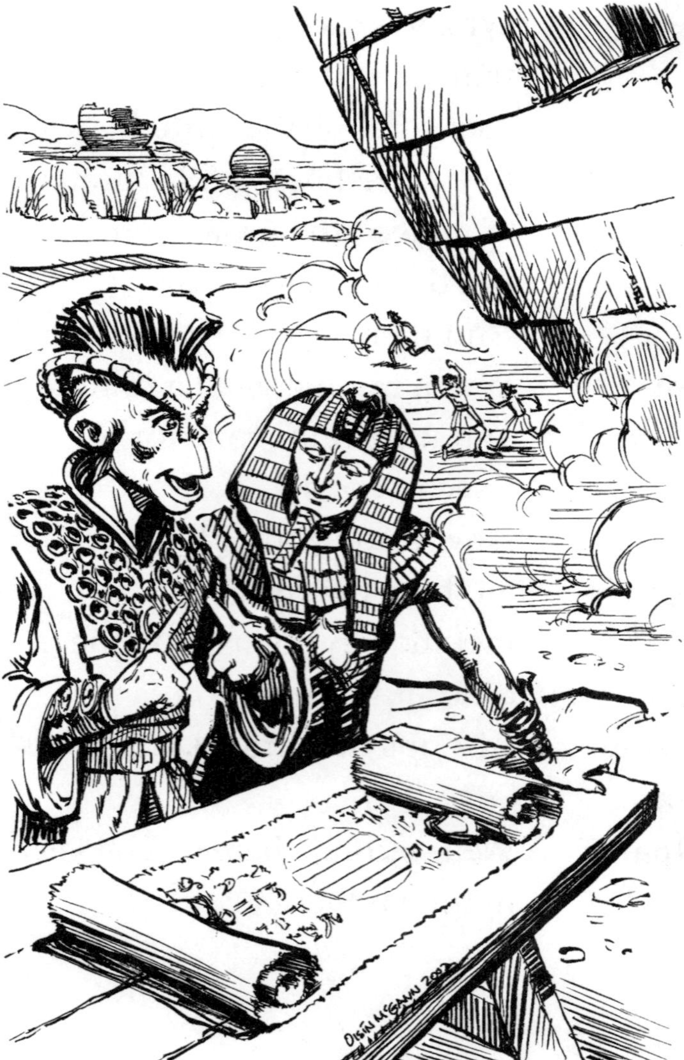

	Look, if . . . Oh, what's the point?
	You wouldn't understand it.
	The thing is, though,
	while I was talking to your Kate,
	I suddenly thought —
Alan	Kate? I don't know any Kate.
Kolpan	Oh I'm sorry,
	you haven't met her yet, have you?
	But you will.
	Next year on a desert island.
Alan	A desert island?
Kolpan	Yes! You and her were . . .
	(chuckling to himself)
	Heh, heh, heh! You and her were . . .
	Well, we won't go into that now.
	Perhaps you're right.
	It's best not to go into the future
	if you're not used to it.
	But as I said, I had this
	sudden thought:
	'Where are all the tourists?'

Alan What?
Kolpan Well, if we set up
a tourist business here –
you and me, like we were saying –
then in a few years' time,
there should be thousands
of Kads and Zirgs
and everybody all over the place.
But there wasn't. Not one.

Alan Wait a minute.
Let me get this straight.
You went into the future
to see if this tourist business –
which we haven't set up yet –
was going to be a success or not?

Kolpan Of course!
That's what we use time travel for.
There's no point
in setting something up
that's going to be a failure.
That would be a real
waste of time.

Alan All right, I think I understand.
But there were no tourists?

Kolpan No.

Alan So we don't set up the business?

Kolpan No. But why not?
That's what I don't understand.
The place is just right,
there's no one else from space
around, and . . . wait a minute.

	What did you say earlier on? Something about little green men?
Alan	Yes, some people say they've seen them, and they're from space.
Kolpan	Oh no . . . They don't have big bug eyes, do they?
Alan	They do, as a matter of fact.
Kolpan	And they don't come in flying saucers?
Alan	Yes! How did you know that?
Kolpan	Oh no! I've got to get out of here now!

He starts to run to his spaceship, but it's too late!
A flying saucer appears next to it, a hatch opens, and a little green man comes out.

All right, officer! I know, I'm sorry!
It's a non-parking zone.
But I just didn't see the signs.

The little green man points something at Kolpan . . .

Oh, you're not going to zap me, just for that?

. . . and presses it.
There's a flash,
and Kolpan and his spaceship disappear.

Alan Hey! What have you done to
Kolpan?
You can't . . .

The little green man points at Alan,
and squeezes again.
There is another flash,
and the flying saucer
and the little green man disappears.

Oh, what was that?
That was bright.
I feel all dizzy.
It must have been the sun.

He shakes his head as if to clear it.

That's better.
Now, where was I?
Where are those maggots?